Essential Tropical Fish

Setup and Maintenance Guide

Anne Finlay

Essential Tropical Fish: Setup & Maintenance

Copyright © 2018 Elluminet Press

This work is subject to copyright. All rights are reserved by the Publisher, whether the whole or part of the material is concerned, specifically the rights of translation, reprinting, reuse of illustrations, recitation, broadcasting, reproduction on microfilms or in any other physical way, and transmission or information storage and retrieval, electronic adaptation, computer software, or by similar or dissimilar methodology now known or hereafter developed. Exempted from this legal reservation are brief excerpts in connection with reviews or scholarly analysis or material supplied specifically for the purpose of being entered and executed on a computer system, for exclusive use by the purchaser of the work. Duplication of this publication or parts thereof is permitted only under the provisions of the Copyright Law of the Publisher's location, in its current version, and permission for use must always be obtained from the Publisher. Permissions for use may be obtained through Rights Link at the Copyright Clearance Centre. Violations are liable to prosecution under the respective Copyright Law.

Trademarked names, logos, and images may appear in this book. Rather than use a trademark symbol with every occurrence of a trademarked name, logo, or image we use the names, logos, and images only in an editorial fashion and to the benefit of the trademark owner, with no intention of infringement of the trademark.

The use in this publication of trade names, trademarks, service marks, and similar terms, even if they are not identified as such, is not to be taken as an expression of opinion as to whether or not they are subject to proprietary rights.

Fish Images used with permission under CCASA / CC-BY-SA-3.0 Luminescent Media.

While the advice and information in this book are believed to be true and accurate at the date of publication, neither the authors nor the editors nor the publisher can accept any legal responsibility for any errors or omissions that may be made. The publisher makes no warranty, express or implied, with respect to the material contained herein.

Publisher: Elluminet Press
Director: Kevin Wilson
Lead Editor: Mike Smith
Copy Editors: Joanne Taylor
Proof Reader: Robert Price
Indexer: James Marsh
Cover Designer: Kevin Wilson

eBook versions and licenses are also available for most titles. Any source code or other supplementary materials referenced by the author in this text is available to readers at

`www.elluminetpress.com/resources`

For detailed information about how to locate your book's source code, go to

`www.elluminetpress.com/resources`

Table of Contents

About the Author

Anne Finlay has had a life long fascination with tropical fish from an early age, starting off with keeping gold fish then moving on to tropical and marine fish.

This led to studying them further at college and working at a public aquarium maintaining the tanks and advising people on the various species.

Her experience of the hobby and the fish trade keeps her abreast of the latest developments and has become the basis for writing this book.

Fish are fascinating to watch and hope you enjoy them as much as we have.

Acknowledgements

Thanks to all the staff at Luminescent Media & Elluminet Press for their passion, dedication and hard work in the preparation and production of this book.

To all my friends and family for their continued support and encouragement in all my writing projects.

Basic Equipment

In this chapter we will take a look at different types of tanks available. You can choose from a variety of different sizes and shapes. Although I find a rectangular one is best for the fish.

We also take a look at all the equipment you will need, such as filters, nets, heaters, lights, pumps and siphons you will need to set up and maintain your tank.

There are rough guides to point you in the right direction when buying a tank, sizes of filters needed, types of heaters, that will help you to get the best out of your tank once you have fish

Plus some specific tools such as nets, scissors and tweesers that are designed to make maintaining your tank and setting it up easier.

Tanks

Fish tanks come in all shapes and sizes. Some are orbs others are cubes and rectangular.

The shape and size of the tank you choose depends on the size and type of fish you want to keep.

If you want to keep larger fish or a lot of fish and you have space a large rectangular tank that matches your furniture can become a great feature in any living room like the one pictured above. This one is 4 foot in length and holds about 275 litres of water and can house large fish such as plecos, clown loaches, angels, discus, etc.

If you want to keep small guppies, neons or tetras a small bio-orb will look nice. Also good if you have limited space.

If you plan to keep larger fish (eg more than 6 inches) then 250litre+ is a good size. Makes a stunning addition to any living room and should be positioned where it can be seen and appreciated.

Think carefully where the tank will be positioned as it weighs a ton when completely full, and would be virtually impossible to move later without draining it or stripping out the decor.

The ideal place would be away from sources of noise such as TVs, radios, washing machines and fridges. Constant exposure to noise and vibrations from these devices will stress the fish out.

Aquariums should be kept away from heaters, fires and radiators which influence the temperature of the water temperature. Most fish need to be kept at a constant temperature

Avoid putting your aquarium windows/skylights or in conservatories. Too much sunlight will cause problems with your water quality and promote the rapid growth of algae.

Always make sure you get a cabinet that is specially designed to support your size aquarium. Water is very heavy and a tank positioned on an unstable cabinet is dangerous and can collapse.

Filters

There are generally two types of filter: Internal and external.

Internal filters stick on the inside wall of the aquarium and are suitable for small to medium sized aquariums.

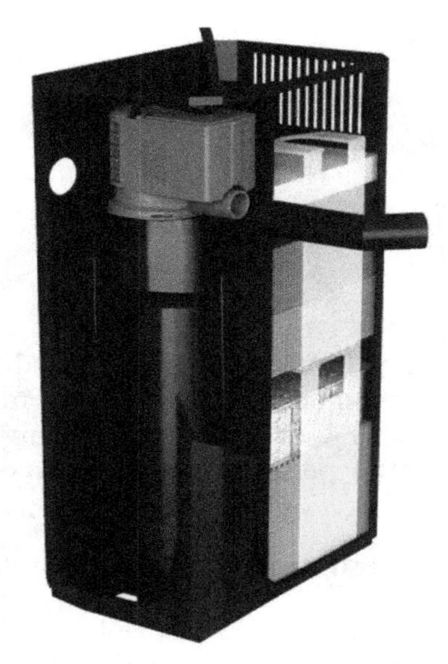

They house all the filter media; sponges and ceramic chips inside the filter unit.

They tend to take up space inside the tank and can be a bit awkward to clean since you have to take the whole thing out the tank to do it. So anything over 60-90 litres you are better opting for an external filter.

External canister filters sit in the cabinet under the aquarium and have pipe work running to and from the tank.

They house all the filter media away from the aquarium making it easy access to clean and allows more space inside the tank. These are best for large tank set-ups. So anything over about 100 litres you would get better performance from an external filter.

What Size Filter?

The packaging will tell you what aquarium size the filter is capable of supporting. Look for a filter that is capable of running a tank at least as large as yours, ideally a bit bigger. If you keep messy fish, such as goldfish or cichlids, or a tank with a lot of fish, you'll need to consider something bigger – the next filter model up.

Below is a table of rough recommendations for filters according to tank volume. I have used the Fluval filters in this guide but any equivalent filter will be sufficient.

Tank Volume	Filter
55 ltr	250ltr/h (eg Fluval U1)
56-90 ltr	400ltr/h (eg Fluval U2)
91-130 ltr	600ltr/h (eg Fluval U3 or 106)
131-150 ltr	800ltr/h (eg Fluval U4 or 206)
151-200 ltr	1000ltr/h (eg Fluval 306)
201-300 ltr	1500ltr/h (eg Fluval 406)
300-500+ ltr	2000ltr/h (eg Fluval FX5)

Keep a note of the estimated litre/hour (ltr/h). This is the amount of water the filter will circulate in one hour. The larger the tank and the more fish the higher rating you will need.

Heaters

Heaters are used to heat the aquarium water to the correct temperature. Most have a dial on the top to allow you to change this according to the requirements of the fish you want to keep.

As a general guide you should have at least 1 watt per 1 litre. So a tank that holds 200 litres (52 US gallons) should be equipped with at least a 200W heater.

The water in the tank is also subject to room temperature variance meaning if your tank is in a cold room, you may need to go for the next model up as you will need more power to keep the water up to temperature.

Below is a table of rough recommendations for heaters based on tank volume in litres.

Volume	Heater
25-49l	50w
50-74l	75w
75-99l	75w (100w in cold room)
100-149l	100w (150w in cold room)
150-199l	150w (200w in cold room)
200-249l	200w (250w in cold room)
250-299l	250w (300w in cold room)
300-399l	300w (use two in cold room)
Over 400l	Two 300w (one at each end)

Lights

To provide enough light for plants to grow and for the fish to feel comfortable, the aquarium should be lit between 5 and 10 hours depending on plant and fish species.

Don't keep your lights on for more than 10 hours as this can cause a lot of green algae to grow. Try to turn the lights on and off at the same times each day to try to simulate a tropical day.

Fluorescent Tubes

T8 tubes are considered standard lighting, if you have a planted aquarium or have a deep aquarium you would need several T8 tubes.

T5 tubes are the brightest fluorescent lighting available but because of this they will also use more electricity and the tubes also get hotter.

LED Lighting

LEDs are cheaper to run as they don't use as much electricity and they come in a wide range of colours, do not emit much heat.

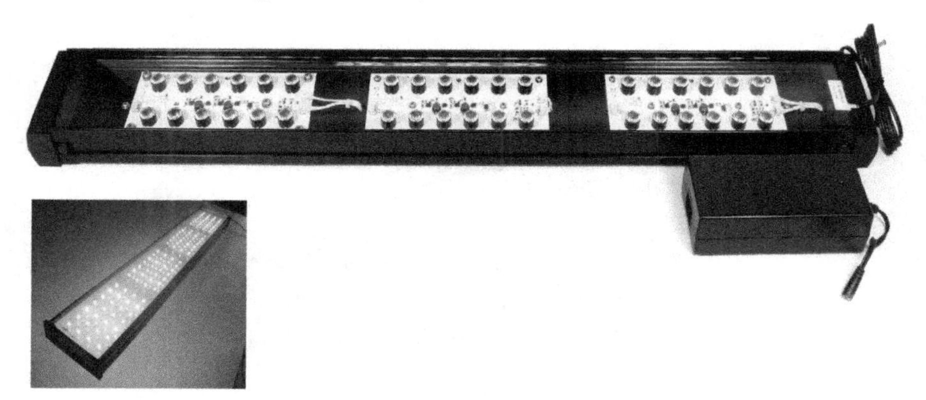

They also last longer, some manufacturers rate them at 30,000 to 50,000 hours. So in theory those lights rated at 30,000 hours won't have to be replaced for 7 years if you ran your lights 12 hours a day. Compare that to replacing a metal halide or T5 bulb every 9-12 months.

Metal Halide

Metal halide lamps are often used over reef tanks as they produce a very high light output but often use more electricity and can produce excessive heat.

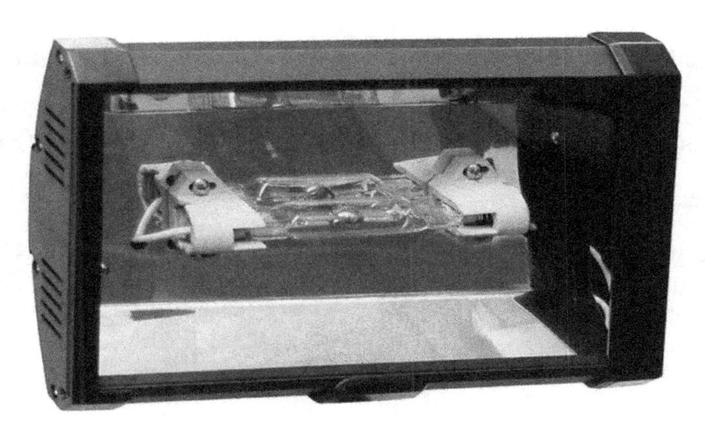

These lights are only really necessary in reef aquariums where high intensity lights are needed and for plants that need strong lights.

How Much Light?

As a very rough guide, I have found the following guidelines provide best plant growth.

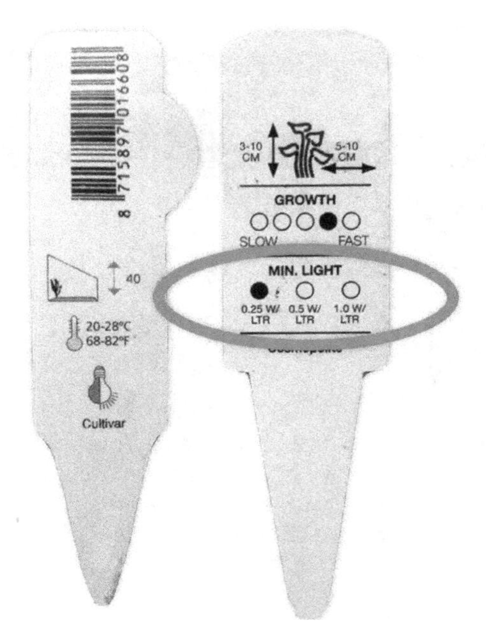

Low lights are between 1 - 2 watts per US gallon (0.3 - 0.5 watt/litre)

Medium lights are between 2 - 3 watts per US gallon (0.5 - 0.8 watt/ litre)

High lights have 3 watts per US gallon or higher (0.8 watt/litre or higher)

Keep these figures in mind when buying plants as it will tell you

For example

250 litre tank @ 0.3 watts per litre. 250×0.3=75w. I put 2, 40watt T8 bulbs in my lighting strip giving me 80watts of light which is enough for most aquatic plants on the market.

60 litre tank @ 0.3 watts per litre. 60×0.3=18w. An 18w-20w T8 or T5 tube will be sufficient.

Remember to measure the length of your tank to make sure the lights fit – especially for smaller tanks and non-rectangular tanks.

Water Conditioners

There are a lot of water conditioners on the market but I have found that API Stress Coat works well with tropical fish.

Water conditioners are designed to make tap water safe for fish. Water companies add chlorine or chloramine to kill pathogens and bacteria in the water to make it fit for human consumption. Unfortunately this isn't good news for fish as chlorine, chloramine and some dissolved heavy metals are toxic to fish, so it's vital to buy a good water conditioner.

When buying a conditioner make sure it neutralises chloramine and chlorine as well as heavy metals from the water, this will usually be stated on the label.

Some conditioners have extra agents that help the fish. Stress Coat contains aloe vera and helps reduce stress in the fish when they have been transported or disturbed during a water change or tank maintenance. Aloe vera also helps to heal gills and fins.

It is also a good idea to keep some ammonia and nitrite remover in case of emergencies especially when your tank has not been running very long.

When you add fish it is possible to get an ammonia spike until the filter bacteria compensates for the extra bioload.

Only use ammonia or nitrite remover if fish are severely stressed and you have performed a water change.

Siphons

Siphon allows you to vacuum up muck from gravel at bottom of the tank into a bucket. This is usually done while 'changing water'. Make sure you get one long enough to reach the bottom of your tank without putting your hands under the water.

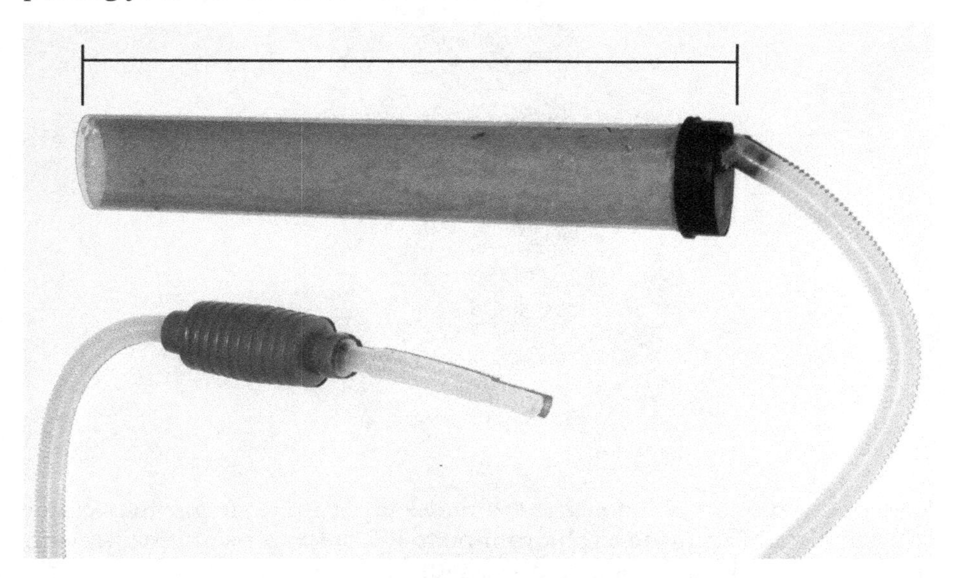

Siphon off the water into a bucket.

Pumps

For large tanks a water pump to pump the prepared and conditioned water back into the tank.

This will save you having to lift a large bucket full of water, which will be extremely heavy.

Rocks & Décor

You can pick up a nice selection of artificial rocks, caves and interesting objects from your local fish store. These can look very real when surrounded by live plants, bog wood and rocks.

Little rocks and caves provide plenty of shelter and hiding places for the fish. This makes them feel more secure in their environment.

Loach tubes are great for bottom dwelling fish such as loaches, plecos and corys. They love to hide in the tubes.

Can you see the loach's nose in the bottom tube? He loves it.

Substrate & Gravel

The choice of gravel and substrate depends greatly on the type of fish you want to keep and whether you want to keep live plants or artificial. I would strongly recommend live plants as it has a lot more benefits to the aquarium than artificial plants.

For bottom dwelling fish you would be better with a fine substrate.

Fine sand is not recommended for live plants as it compacts the roots cutting off nutrients and can cause problems.

For live plants it is good to put it down in the tank in layers. The first layer could be something like Eco Complete Planting Substrate which contains Iron, calcium, magnesium, potassium, sulphur plus over 25 other elements.

This contains all the mineral nutrients needed for luxurious aquatic plant growth without nuisance algae. It will not increase pH or carbonate hardness. No artificial dyes, paints or chemical coatings. Encourages the most vibrant colouration in fishes and reduces stress. Supplies calcium without raising pH. Contains live Heterotrophic bacteria to rapidly convert your fishes waste into natural food for your aquatic plants.

Tetra Plant Complete Substrate is another substrate specially formulated planting medium, for long-term fertilisation.

It creates ideal environment for aquatic plants, ensuring long-term release of key nutrients. Contains high quality mix of sand and black peat, with high iron and trace element content. Optimum grain size for rapid development of healthy roots. Free of nitrates and phosphates to prevent algae growth.

There are plenty more on the market but I find either of these ones are fine for the bottom layer.

For the top layer, this is personal choice but I would recommend a dark brown fine gravel with 1mm grains. This will give it the most natural look and will show up the green plants well against the dark brown gravel. For example JBL Manado. Any fine gravel or course sand will do.

Fine gravel is also much better for bottom dwelling fish such as loaches and corys as they love to dig into the gravel for food.

Again this is personal taste but coloured gravels I think ruin the look of a planted aquarium.

I believe a dark brown or even light brown colour highlights the plants and enhances the colours of the fish.

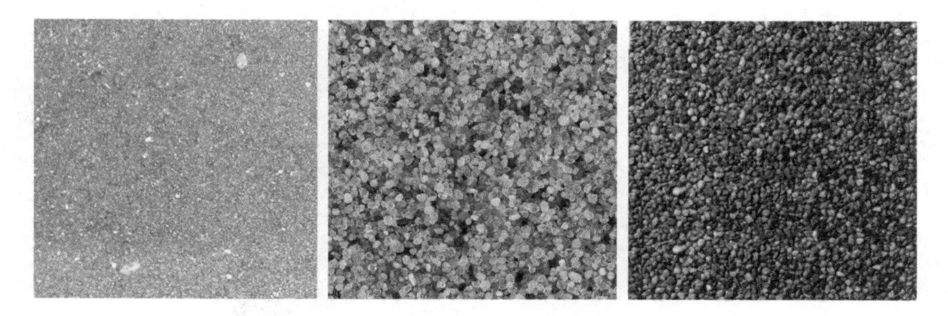

Any of the above types of gravel will do. These ones I have found to offer the best for both live plants and bottom dwelling fish such as loaches and corries.

Driftwood & Bogwood

These types of wood must be thoroughly cleaned and soaked in boiling water for a few days before they are ready for the aquarium.

Bogwood or Mopani wood is a great addition to any aquarium and is vital if you have plecos in your tank. They love to gnaw at the wood.

To prepare bogwood or Mopani wood you must first give it a scrub with hot water only.

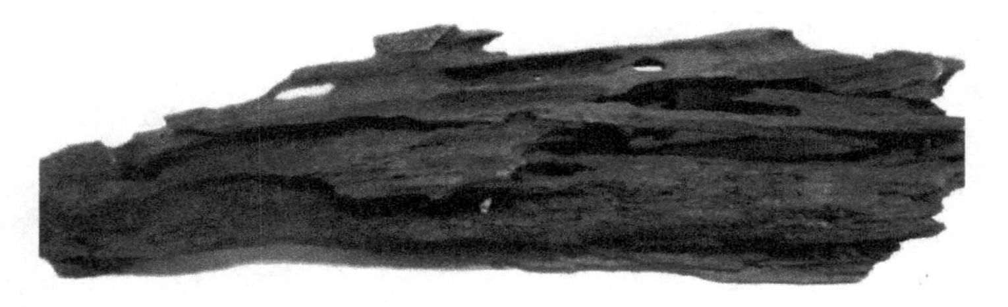

Then once you have done that soak it in a bucket of boiling water for about 3 days.

You will need to replace the water every day until it is clear.

You can also attach some cool plants to your wood such as anubias or java fern.

The fish love to swim through it and inspect the leaves and it makes a nice addition to the tank.

Other Tools

Long handle tweezers for picking things up from the bottom of the tank

Cutters for trimming off leaves on live plants without having to put your hands and arms in the water

Fish nets. One with a long handle, makes handling fish a lot easier. Select the size of the net depending on the size of fish you get.

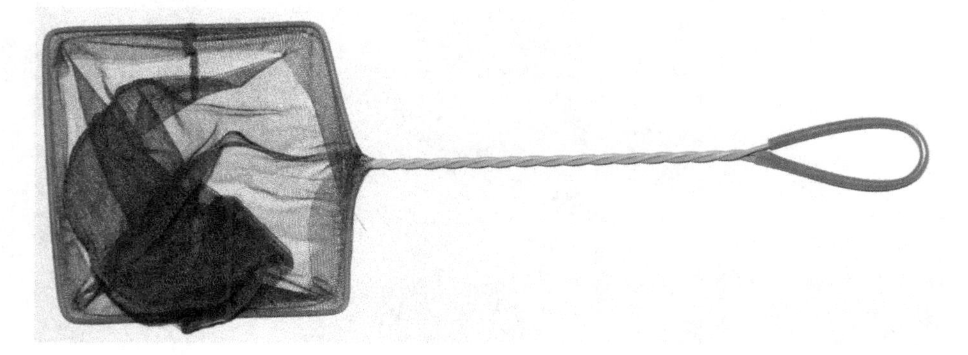

Something to keep the inside of the glass clean from algae. A magnetic algae cleaner or an algae sponge pad with a long pole handle to save you putting your hands in the tank. These can be great for cleaning the inside of the glass, don't clean too far down as you will disturb all the substrate on the bottom and it could pick up some of the substrate and scratch the glass. Leave the bottom bits for a bristlenose plec.

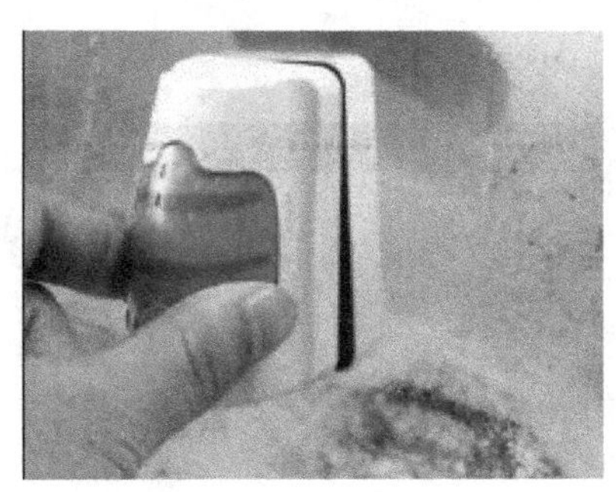

Air Pumps

Little air pumps allow you to create some great looking effects with air stones and bubble walls.

All you need to get is an air pump, some silicone tubing, an airstone or bubble wall and a non-return valve to stop the water syphoning out your tank through the tubing.

The size of your pump depends on the size of your air stone or bubble wall.

The columns in the table below, you need to take note of is the size of your air wall and the air flow and get a pump with the appropriate airflow for the size of feature.

Model	Powers filters in aquariums up to approx.		Size of Airwall		Max no. of other features	Air Flow (L/hr)	Pressure (mbar)
AVMINI	46cm (18″ long)	OR	1 x 1″ Airstone	OR	1	75	0.22
AV1	60cm (24″ long)	OR	1 x 12″ Airwall	OR	2	170	0.23
AV2	100cm (36″ long)	OR	1 x 18″ Airwall	OR	4	200	0.27
AV3	120cm (48″ long)	OR	4 x 12″ Airwall	OR	6	2 x 250	0.23
AV4	150cm (60″ long)	OR	4 x 18″ Airwall	OR	8	2 x 300	0.23

These are manufacturer's recommendations and are usually exaggerated and if you want to run bubble walls or air stone ornaments some air pumps are rated for different sizes of tanks, but these ratings are, actually, nearly irrelevant to choosing the correct air pump.

For example, the AVMINI above will be sufficient for up to a 30cm air wall and the ornaments shown above.

Tanks deeper than 50cm or much bigger ornaments might need more air flow, eg next model up. Check the air flow rating on the side of the ornaments/airwall you want to install.

You don't want to end up with too much air flow as it will create too powerful a bubble wall which is not good for some types of fish and will quickly deplete any CO_2 in planted tanks.

Air pumps are not really recommended for planted tanks as they have a tendency to drive off dissolved CO_2 in the water required for good aquatic plant growth.

Setting Up Your Tank

This is where the fun begins, where we can begin to build our tank. First make sure you have positioned it in the place where you know it will stay as a full tank is ridiculously heavy and is difficult and dangerous to move.

It is also a good idea to make sure the cabinet is strong enough to hold the weight.

I would place it in a position where you can most enjoy watching the fish, say in a living room where you can sit and watch.

Once you have decided that we can get started unpacking and putting the tank together.

Install Filter & Heater

Once you have your tank positioned on a stable cabinet in the place where you want it, begin to build the tank. Add your filter, install it according to the manufacturer's instructions. If it's an internal filter place it in the back right hand corner as shown below. This will give the best water circulation.

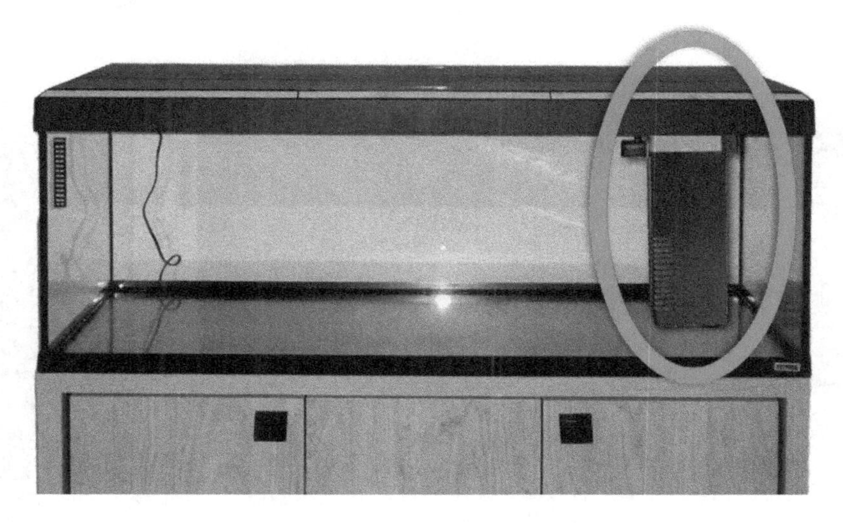

Next place the heater in the opposite back corner of the tank as shown above. Make sure your heater doesn't touch anything that will be going in the tank such as rocks or substrate. This can cause the glass on the heater to crack.

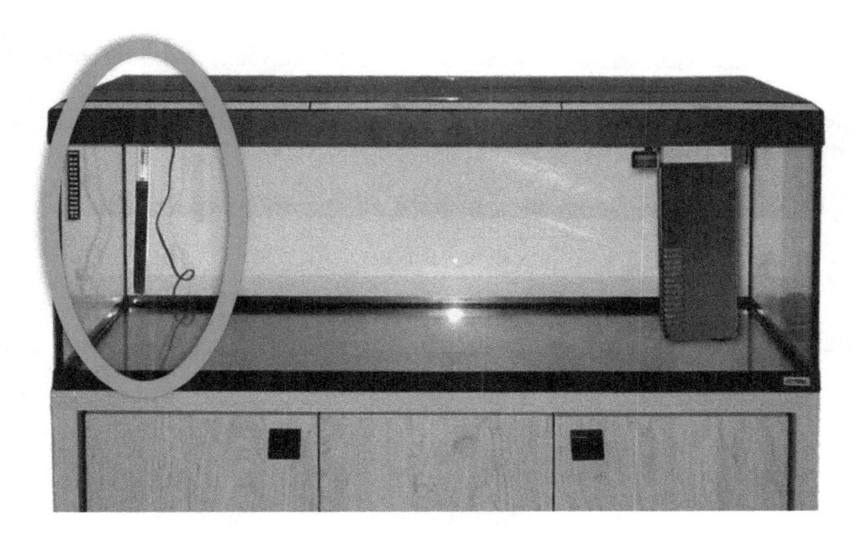

Lights

Install the lights in the hood according to the manufacturer's instructions. Do not turn anything on (except the lights) at this point. The heater & filter can only work under water.

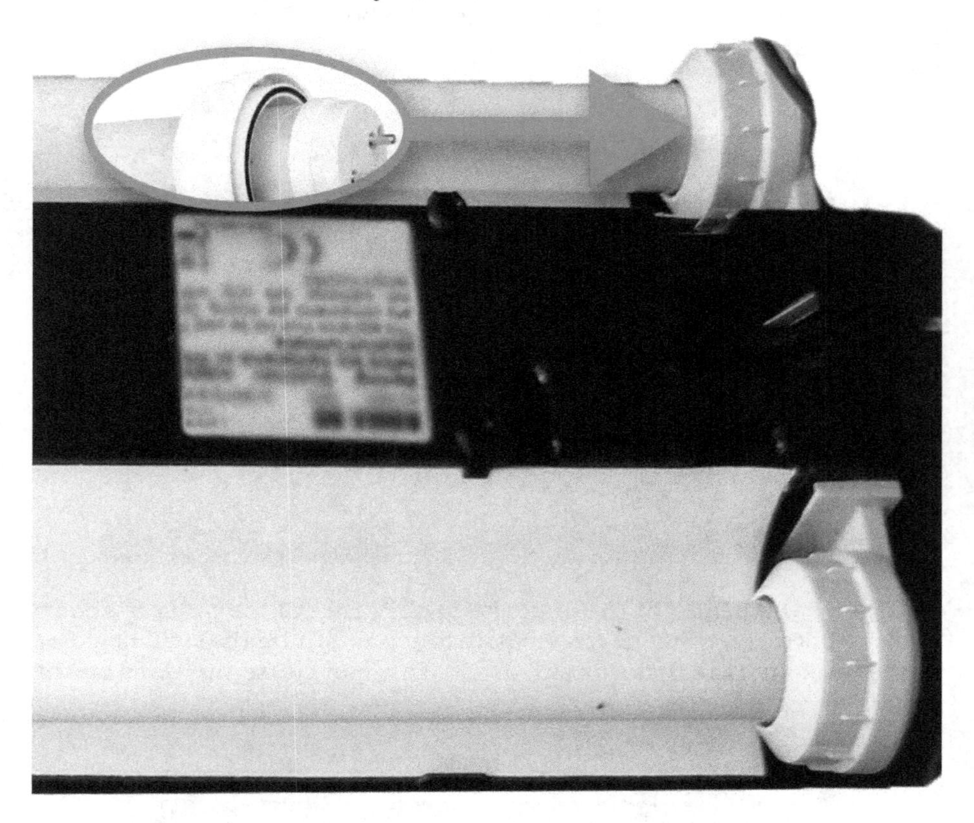

Slide the waterproof seal caps along the fluorescent tube with the seal facing out as illustrated above.

Slot the tubes into the metal contacts on the light fitting.

Slide the waterproof seal caps to the end until they clip in place. Some models you will have to turn the caps until they screw into place.

Make sure there is a waterproof seal around the tube to keep water out.

Add the Substrate & Gravel

Add your planting substrate to the bottom (such as tetra plant complete). Do not wash the bottom layer of planting substrate.

Level the substrate off into a nice bed so it covers the whole area. Make sure you have 2-3" to enable plant roots to take hold.

Next you will need to cover the planting substrate with some kind of aquarium gravel. Fine gravel such as JBL Monado usually works best with live plants. Aquarium gravels usually need rinsing before use otherwise it will make the water very cloudy. Rinse the gravel in a bucket a bit at a time. Make sure you get most of the dust off.

Once you have done that scoop the gravel out of the water in the bucket and place it over the planting substrate in the tank.

You should have about an inch or two layer on top of the substrate. You can see in the photo below a layer of planting substrate at the bottom and a layer of gravel over the top.

When you have put all the gravel over the top, level it out into a nice bed. If you prefer, the gravel doesn't have to be flat, you can create little hills or make the back higher than the front, it's completely up to you.

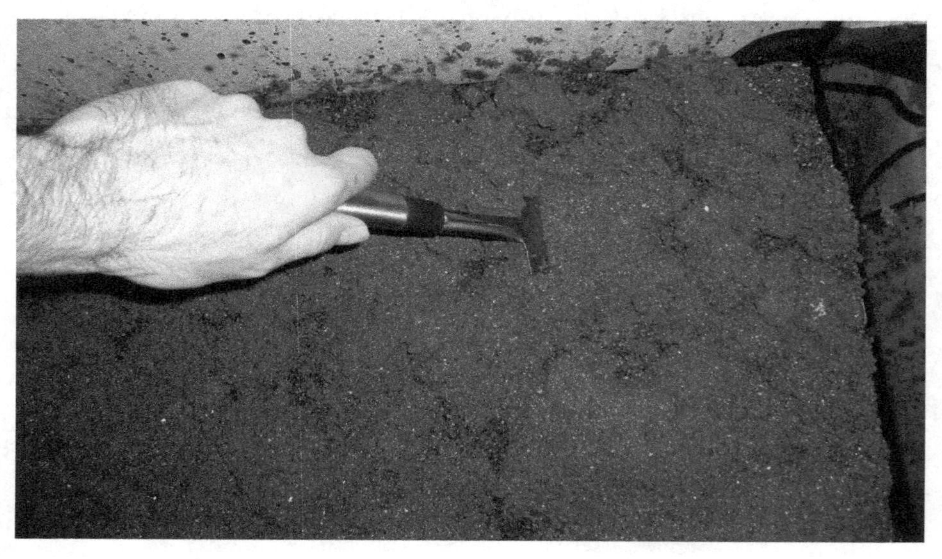

Adding Rocks & Décor

Make sure you give them a good clean with hot water only before putting them in. Lay them nicely across the bed, making the best use of the space. Make sure you leave space behind and in between them for plants. Leave the front section for small items.

Little rocks and caves provide plenty of shelter and hiding places for the fish. This gives them shelter and makes them feel more secure in their environment.

Fill the tank with water only to about 2 inches above the surface of the substrate, take care not to disturb the substrate too much. Use a dinner plate to help

The idea of just filling the tank a couple of inches makes it easier to plant your plants. Working at arm's length in a tank full of water is more difficult.

Plant your Plants

Some good examples of plants to start off with that are popular.

- Cryptocorynes, Echinodorus (sword plants),
- Egeria Densa (anacharis),
- Hornwort,
- Java Moss,
- Java Fern,
- Ludwigia,
- Rotalas,
- Water sprite,
- Hygrophilas (water wisteria and brethren),
- Marsilea sp (water clover).

Place taller plants at the back such as amazon sword and shorter plants at the front such as anubias nana or wheat plant.

Arrange your larger plants across the back and sides taking care not to block the filter. This will provide ample swimming space across the centre front of the tank. Smaller plants at the front.

Try combining plants with different leaf shapes and shades – dark green, light green etc

Make sure you plant them in groups rather than dotting individual plants around the tank and allow room to grow.

Carefully remove the plant from its little pot and take all the rock wool from around the roots. Also check in there for snails.

Plant the roots about an inch into the substrate, take care not to bury too much of the stems (or crown) as it may rot. Just bury the roots.

Depending on the type of plant, sometimes it is useful to weight them down with lead weights. These are readily available in most aquarium stores and should be loosely wrapped around the plant as not to choke it or break the roots as it grows.

For anubias nana and java fern, it is best to attach these to a rock, tank ornament or a piece of driftwood as they tend to rot if planted in the substrate.

You may need to tie the plant on at first with a piece of nylon thread or fine fishing line until the roots get a hold for themselves.

Once you are happy with the layout of your tank you can start to fill the tank with water to the maximum fill line.

As suggested earlier, place a large dinner plate over the substrate so the water doesn't disturb the bottom.

Fill the tank to the top using either a hose pipe or buckets.

Don't fill the tank above the maximum fill line.

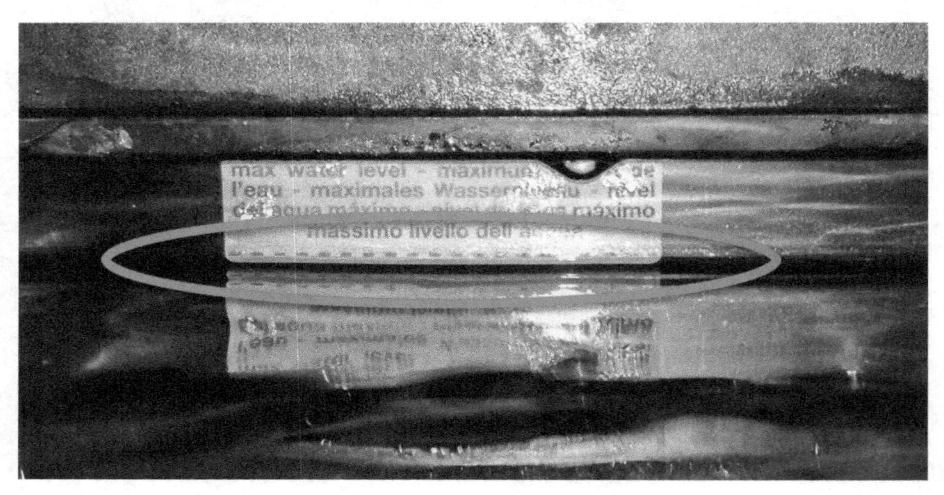

Once the tank is full, add the correct dose of water conditioner. This will be labelled on the bottle

Now we have a full tank, we can start to cycle it and prepare for the fish.

Preparing your Tank for Fish

Before you rush out and buy your fish you need to prepare your tank first.

The water must be at the correct temperature and you need to let the tank mature and build up the ability to convert fish waste (such as ammonia and nitrite) into something less toxic.

This is called cycling your tank and is the process of building up bacteria in the filter sponges and on the surfaces of the tank. This bacteria break down and remove the toxic ammonia secreted by the fish.

Without this process the ammonia from the fish waste will quickly build up in the water and poison the fish. This is a common problem with new tanks and has been dubbed “new tank syndrome”.

The Nitrogen Cycle

The nitrogen cycle is the process whereby ammonia secreted by animals as waste, is converted by bacteria to nitrite and then into nitrate.

Note the spellings: nitr**ite** is the toxic one. Nitr**ate** is far less toxic

Ammonia and nitr**ite** are highly toxic to fish in very low concentrations, so establishing the bacteria colonies that quickly convert these compounds to nitrate is crucial to creating a healthy environment for fish. Nitr**ate** is far less toxic, and can easily be removed through periodic water changes or consumption by live plants. Most fish that die in new tanks can be traced back to the lack of an established nitrogen cycle in the tank.

Fish excrete urea, which contains ammonia. In a new tank that does not have the necessary bacteria colonies, this ammonia will rapidly accumulate to the point where it is lethal to the fish.

So cycling your tank is the process of establishing the bacterial colonies which will be mostly in the filter media but will also coat all the walls and rocks in the aquarium.

The bacteria will also grow in the substrate, this is why it's important to have a good quality substrate as the bacteria colonies will grow and help consume toxins from fish waste and uneaten food that falls to the floor of the tank. This is the secret to maintaining a healthy clean fish tank.

Cycling the Tank

All it takes to some kind of an ammonia source. Pure ammonia available in most home improvement stores or Garden shops and is sometimes labelled as ammonium hydroxide. If using this option, make sure the ammonia is free of any surfactants, dyes or perfumes as they may poison the fish in long term.

To test for surfactants, just shake the ammonia bottle before purchasing and if it fizzles or gives bubbles then there are surfactants present. Also use only pure ammonia — that is one which is not scented.

Fist get yourself an "ammonia alert" indicator. These can be purchased from any local fish store and usually last a month or two.

This can be stuck to the inside of the glass in the tank and will help you to monitor the amount of ammonia you add to the tank.

Put a few drops of pure ammonia in the tank - enough ammonia to turn the "Ammonia Alert" dark (toxic). Wait for the ammonia alert to go back to a "safe" level. This may take several days.

Continue to add ammonia to the tank until the "Ammonia alert" indicator shows that the ammonia level goes back to the safe level within 8-12 hours after the ammonia is put in. This process can take a couple of weeks.

Once the tank shows the ability to lower the ammonia level in this time interval, this means that a large population of bacteria is resident in your filter. The first stage is complete.

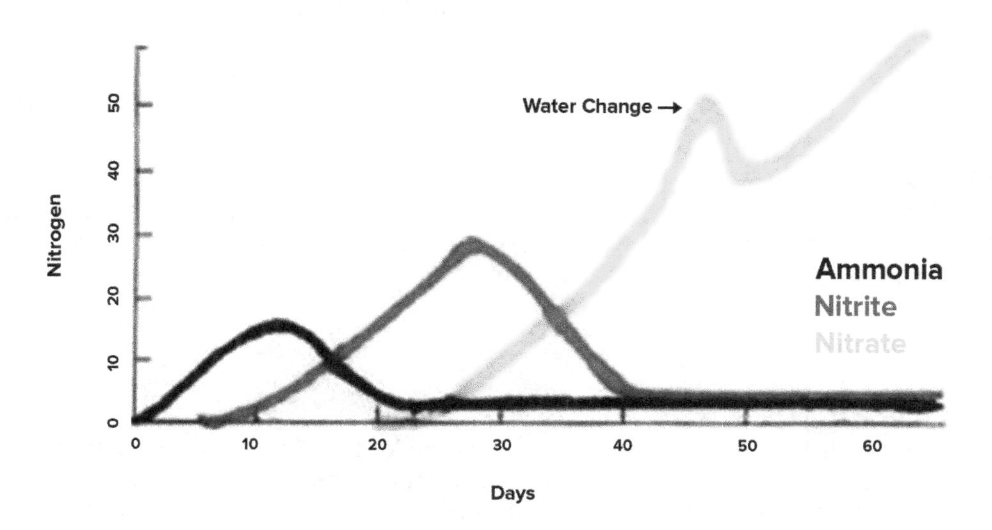

While the ammonia alert indicator is showing safe, use your test kit and test for nitr**ite** (NO_2).

The reading will be begin to rise at first, then after a few days it will drop. Keep adding your ammonia and test after 8-12 hours. Do this as many times as needed, until both the ammonia and nitrite readings fall to 0.

When you have 0ppm of ammonia, 0 ppm of nitrite, test for nitrate. If all has gone to plan the nitrate reading will be quite high. This is fine because nitrate is the end product of the cycling process and is an indicator that your tank is cycled.

Continue to add a few drops of ammonia to your tank until you add your fish. This will keep the bacteria from dying.

Before adding fish, do a large water change (70-90%) to get your nitrate under 40ppm.

Once the fish are added, continue to test the water for both ammonia and nitrite to ensure that no spikes occur.

Do not add any ammonia once fish are added.

Reference Guide

Here is a reference guide to help you read the api test. The information below will help you gauge where your levels should be as well as understand the results.

pH

NORMAL RANGE: 6.5-8.2
The measure of whether the water is acid or alkaline. Water with a pH less than 7 is acidic while a pH greater than 7 is alkaline. Rapid changes in pH are detrimental to fish.

Chlorine and Chloramine

NORMAL RESULTS: 0.0 mg/L
This is added to city water supplies to make the water supply safe for human consumption. Be certain to always use a water conditioner when adding water to an aquarium because any amount of chlorine is toxic to fish.

Ammonia (NH_3)

NORMAL RESULTS: 0.0-0.25 mg/L
Aquariums with properly operating filtration systems should have no ammonia present (after they have been cycled). In new aquariums, Ammonia Removers can be used to lower ammonia levels, along with partial water changes.

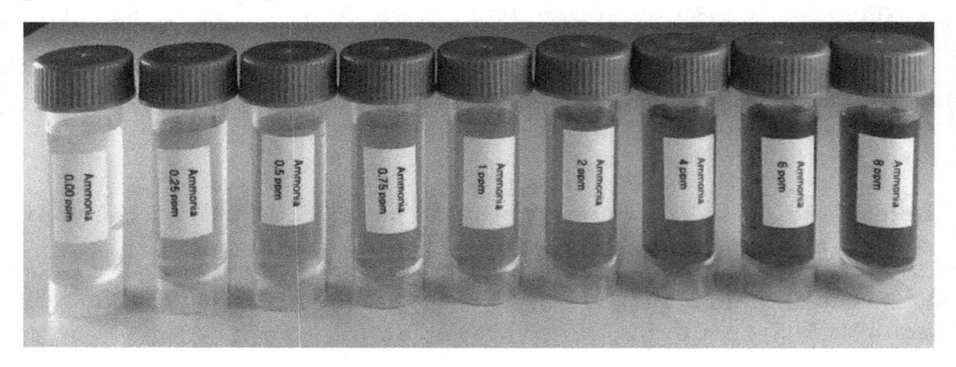

Nitrite (NO_2)

NORMAL RESULTS: 0.0-0.05 mg/L

Nitrite reduces the ability of the fish's blood to carry oxygen. You can remove excess nitrite from an aquarium by performing a partial water change.

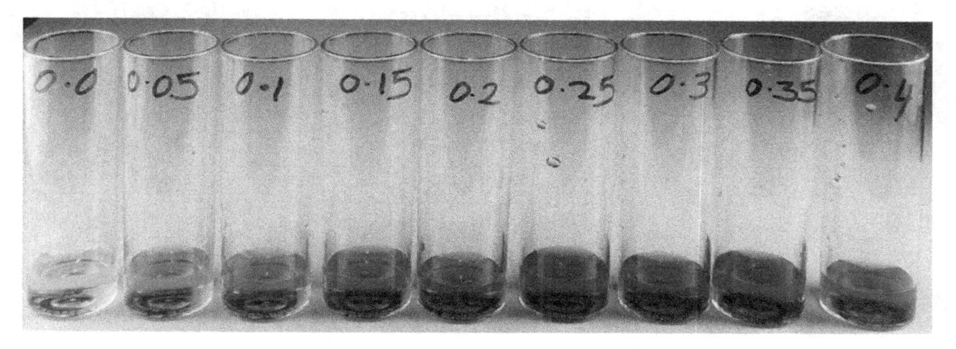

Nitrate (NO_3)

NORMAL RANGE: 0-40 mg/L

If nitrate levels exceed 40 mg/L, water changes can be used to lower the concentration.

High levels of nitrate can also cause increased algae growth.

Carbonate Hardness (KH)

NORMAL RANGE: 3°d-10°d.

KH is the amount of bicarbonate (HCO_3-) and carbonate (CO_3^{2-}) in the water. This is called the buffering capacity of the water and prevents the pH from dropping or changing sharply.

With low KH water, your aquarium may experience sudden and deadly pH shifts. Soft water can be made harder by using calcareous substances such as dolomite which is composed of both calcium and magnesium. Crushed coral, marble and limestone also work but need to be in crushed form to have any effect. The amount required depends on the softness of the original water, but in general, very little calcareous material is required.

In comparison hard water can be made softer by diluting it with reverse osmosis (RO) water, distilled water, and rainwater can be used.

General Hardness (GH)

NORMAL RANGE: 6-12 dH.

This total dissolved minerals such as calcium and magnesium in the water. Plants and fish need both to survive

Degrees	PPM Concentration	Soft/Hard
0 – 4 (dH)	0 - 70 ppm	Very soft
4 – 8 (dH)	70 - 140 ppm	Soft
8 – 12 (dH)	140 - 210 ppm	Medium
12 – 18 (dH)	210 - 320 ppm	Medium-Hard
18 – 30 (dH)	320 - 530 ppm	Hard
30+ (dH)	530 + ppm	Very Hard

Temperature

NORMAL RANGE: 74-82° F (23-28° C)

Use an aquarium heater to maintain stable water temperatures. Rapid temperature changes are harmful to tropical fish.

Adding Fish

There are hundreds of different species to choose from and it is difficult to suggest fish as everyone has different tastes. However there are a few points to consider when choosing your fish.

Beginners and those with new aquariums should start with hardy fish that can tolerate a wide range of water parameters, eg guppies, platies, tetras etc. Loaches, discus, angels etc should only be added to well established tanks.

Selecting Fish

Some are more hardy than others and should only be introduced to an established aquarium. Loaches require pristine water conditions to thrive.

The adult size of the fish should be your first consideration as many species are sold as juveniles and will grow. A fish will eat anything that it thinks it can get in its mouth more often than not this will include small fish and even the fish's babies.

With this in mind, remember that fish that will get big and likely to eat fish that stay small, even if the large fish is generally considered peaceful.

Temperament of the Fish is another thing to consider if you are setting up a community aquarium, that is an aquarium with different species. Some fish are peaceful which means they tend to keep to themselves, some need to be kept in groups, others are ok on their own.

Some are aggressive and territorial and can only be kept on their own.

Keeping aggressive fish with peaceful fish is not recommended. Even if they are the same size - or if the aggressive fish is smaller - the aggressive fish will attack the peaceful fish. Sometimes aggressive fish will keep more peaceful tank mates away from food and chase them, causing the them to die from malnutrition or become more prone to disease due to stress. Keep to the peaceful fish to begin with, these usually make good community tank mates.

How Many Fish Can I Have?

The first step is determining the air surface area of the tank.

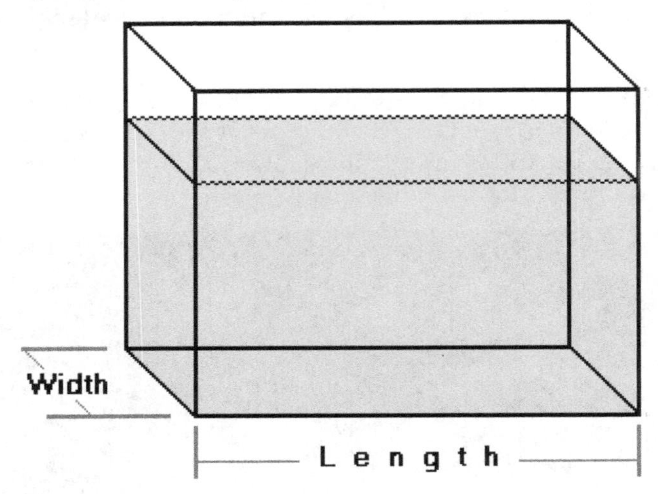

24" x 12" = 288 square inches

Keep in mind when using the size of fish; it has to be the maximum growth the fish will reach.

- For fish the size of grown Guppies, Swordtails, large Platies and fish of about 3", need about *8 square inches per fish (4 x 2 inches).*
- Medium Barbs, 4" in size, and other fish of equal weight should have *20 square inches per fish (4 x 5 inches).*
- Large Barbs and Cichlids of 5-6" length require a minimum of *54 inches per fish (6 x 9 inches).*

So taking our guppy aquarium in the example: 24" x 12" gives us 288 square inches of air surface area. So divide the total air surface area by the number of square inches per fish.

288 ÷ 8 = 36

This tank can safely support 36 grown guppies, giving each over 8 inches of 'elbow room'.

These are minimum requirements and is given as a rough guide, not taking into account plants or filtration and temperature. Use common sense when deciding.

Adding Fish to your Tank

Turn off aquarium lights and dim the lights in the room where the shipping box will be opened. Never open the box in bright light - severe stress or trauma may result from sudden exposure to bright light.

Float the sealed bag in the aquarium for 15 minutes without opening it. This step allows the water in the bag to adjust slowly to the temperature of the aquarium, while maintaining a high level of dissolved oxygen.

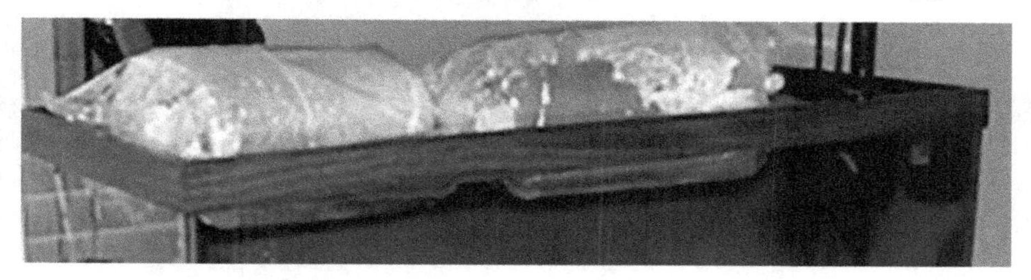

After floating the sealed bag for 15 minutes, cut it open just under the knot or clip and roll open the top of the bag down to create an air pocket within the lip of the bag as shown below.

This will enable the bag to float on the surface of the water.

Gently add 1/2 cup of your aquarium water to the bag.

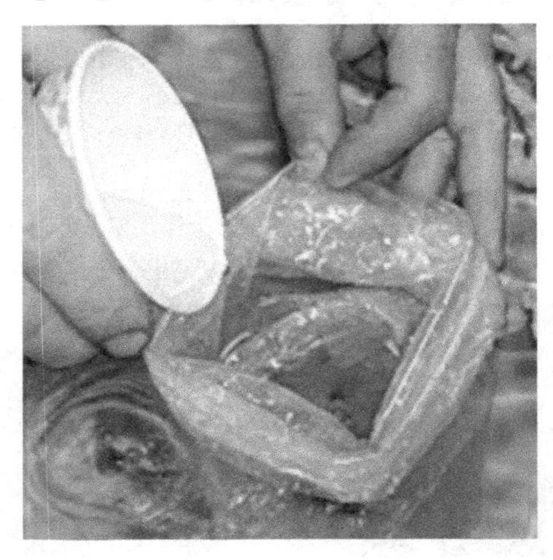

Repeat every ten minutes for about half an hour to an hour. This is to slowly adjust the water chemistry in the bag to match the water in your tank so it is not so much of a shock to the fish. It's like us quickly going from a hot room to the freezing cold outside in a t-shirt.

Gently net your fish from the bag and him release into the aquarium. Be patient and gentle, the fish will be stressed at this point and will try to escape.

Remove the bag from the aquarium. Keep the water handy just in case there is a problem with your fish.

Do not release shipping water directly into the aquarium. This helps prevent the spread of disease and any muck caught in the water from the fish store getting into your tank.

Dose the aquarium with 5ml of stress coat.

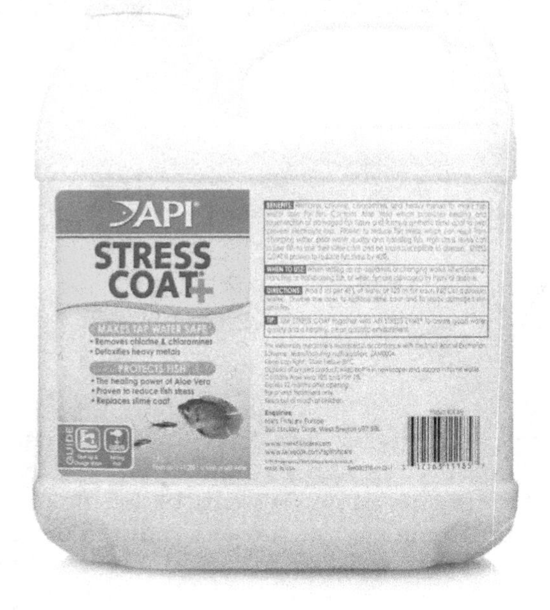

If your fish has settled in then discard the water.

Feeding your Fish

When buying fish food do some research and find out if your fish is an herbivore, a carnivore, or an omnivore. Most fish can be fed flake food or pellets, but some species have specialized diets such as plecs. You may want to buy several types of food.

Feed your fish in small portions, only as much as your fish can eat in 2 or 3 minutes. If you put too much food in the tank, scoop it out with a fine net otherwise it will rot in the tank and pollute the water.

Two or three times a week, give your fish frozen foods, such as bloodworms, tubifex worms, daphnia, or brine shrimp. This will improve their overall health and colour.

You can also supplement their diet with vegetables. Carrots, zucchini/courgette, cucumbers, carrots, lettuce, and peas. You may need to blanch carrots to soften. You can attach a little lead weight to a slice of vegetable such as cucumber and drop it into your tank.

Be sure to remove any uneaten vegetables within 48 hours, or it will start to rot in your tank. Loaches and Plecs always appreciate some fresh veg.

Feeding Time

This is one of my favourite parts, watching the fish feed and feeding them by hand.

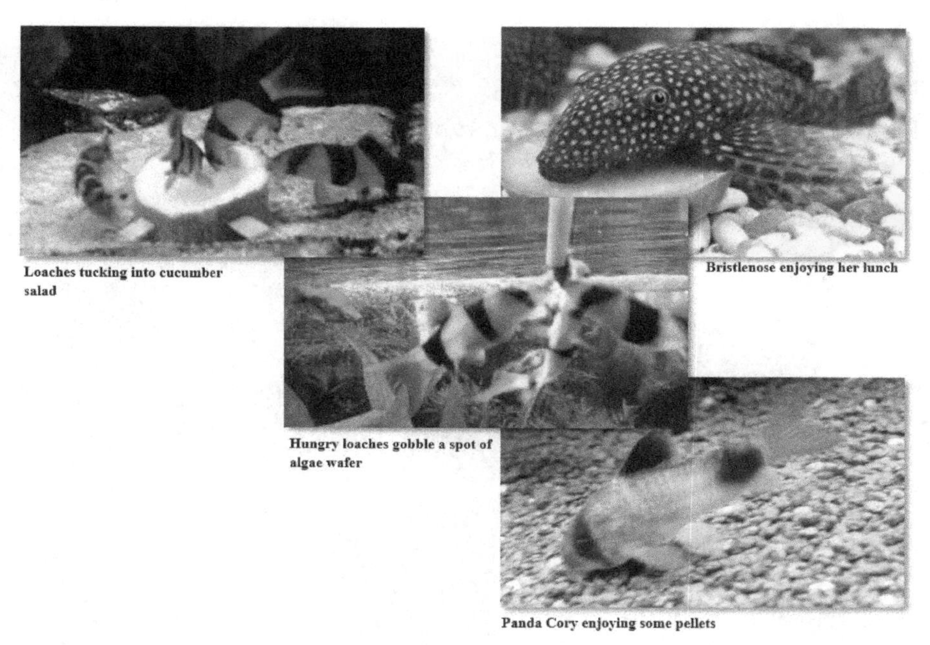

Loaches tucking into cucumber salad

Bristlenose enjoying her lunch

Hungry loaches gobble a spot of algae wafer

Panda Cory enjoying some pellets

I get a lot of enjoyment hand feeding loaches and the other fish. If you use your hands always make sure they are clean and free from hand cream, soaps etc as these can poison the fish.

Get yourself a good set of feeding tongs and use them to dip the food below the surface and watch them feed. The fish love it and by doing it this way the fish become very tame and interact with you more.

As soon as they see you, they start to gather at the top of the aquarium waiting for their food.

Types of Food

The fish's staple diet usually consists of some kind of flake or pellet food and can be supplemented with frozen foods and fresh veg.

Flakes

Floating flakes are ideal for fish that swim near the top or middle of the aquarium, such as guppies, platies, angels, etc

They are available in many varieties but mainly look like the ones pictured.

Bottom dwellers like loaches and corys might get whatever falls to the floor but these are better fed with sinking pellets.

Pellets

For bottom dwellers such as corys and loaches a sinking pellet food would be more suitable for them as it sinks to the bottom allowing these fish to feed naturally from the floor of the tank.

Some pellets can be a bit large for the smaller of the bottom dwellers such as panda corys so you may need to help them out and crush the pellets lightly to make them easier to eat

Wafers

Another good type of food is an algae wafer.

These are also great for bottom dwellers but are especially good for plecos such as bristlenose. You can also get small crip type wafers that are also good for angels and loaches.

Depending on the size of your plec, again you might have to break bits off the algae wafer to feed them as they may not be able to eat a full one and any leftover food will rot.

Frozen Foods

Many fish stores keep frozen foods in a freezer somewhere in the store. You may need to ask for these.

There are many types available and are usually things like bloodworm, daphnia, krill, spirulina etc. They are packaged into blister packs as shown below. The idea is you can use this to gauge how much to feed your fish.

Other Foods

You can also feed your fish fresh veg. Such as cucumber, peas, courgette/zuchini.

Before feeding your fish any vegetable or fruit, you need to rinse thoroughly before cutting up and must be removed within 24-48 hours; otherwise, they will foul up the tank.

Avoid fruit that has a lot of juice, use vegetables that are low in carbohydrates and avoid those high in starchy carbohydrates and sugar such as potatoes and sweet potatoes.

High carbohydrate food may interfere with digestion or nutrient absorption and encourage parasite reproduction and generally pollute the water.

Bristlenose plecs and loaches just love cucumber.

How Much to Feed

This is a difficult question to answer as different fish have different requirements. The rule of thumb is to feed them all they can eat in a couple of minutes. So I would add a few flakes at a time and see if they eat it all, then add a bit more. You don't want any uneaten food left behind as it will rot.

You may need to add a mixture of food, eg, flakes for top feeders mixed with pellets or chips for bottom feeders, so the flakes keep the top feeders busy giving the pellets time to drop to the floor for the bottom feeders, otherwise the more dominant fish will eat anything they can find leaving none for the bottom feeders.

Make sure all the fish receive some.

By doing it this way you will soon get to know the fish's feeding habits and you will be able to gauge how much to feed them without leaving them underfed or leftover food in the tank.

Here is a summary of the different types of food on the market and what type of fish they are suitable for.

Food Format	Water Level	Best For	Notes
Flakes	Floating	Top Feeders	Shortest retention of full vitamin and nutritional content. Replace every month.
Pellets or Sticks	Either sinking or floating	Sinking are good for mid-water feeders; floating good for top feeders	Usually larger; for larger fish
Granules	Either sinking or floating	Sinking are good for mid-water feeders; floating good for top feeders	Essentially smaller pellets
Wafers/Tablets	Sinking	Bottom-feeders and scavengers	Usually made to meet nutrient needs of bottom-feeders

Fish can be carnivorous meaning they eat fish based foods, insects or smaller fish.

They can be herbivorous meaning they eat plants, algae, seaweed etc.

They can also be omnivorous meaning they eat both types of food. This should be taken into account when buying food for your fish.

It's always worth finding out which of the three categories they fall into then buy your food accordingly. Below is a summary of the different diet types.

Diet Type	Restrictions	Popular Example	Natural Diet	Staple Needs (Daily)
Carnivore	Derive no/minimal nutrients from vegetation	Bettas, Discus, Anthias	Smaller fish, invertebrates, crustaceans, insects	Fish-protein based (fish meals, squid meals, shrimp, krill)
Herbivore	Cannot digest meats or most land plants	Otos & Plecos (catfish), some African cichlids, tangs	Live plants, seaweed, algae	Plant-protein based - spirulina, algae, soybean meal
Omnivore	Cannot digest some grains and plants (look for aquatic plants)	Goldfish, Gouramis, Clownfish	A variety of animal and vegetative matter	Balance of meat & plant proteins (a good tropical or marine staple)

Maintaining your Aquarium

Maintaining your tank is the key to keeping healthy fish. Once a week do a water change, always add a conditioner to water if draw from a tap/faucet.

Every month it is a good idea to check and clean your filter and make sure your heater is working. This is important as this is your fish's life support system.

Inspect your fish to make sure they are healthy and no signs of disease. If you spot anything it is best to catch any disease quickly and get the correct treatment.

Also if you have any live plants, make sure they are neatly trimmed and the leaves are a healthy green. Cut off any yellow or brown leaves. You may need to dose with a fertilizer and add some CO_2 to your tank.

In this chapter we will take a look at some strategies for maintaining a healthy tank that I have found useful over the years and hope that it helps you keep your tank in good condition.

Water Changes

Once a week switch off your heater then syphon out 30% of the volume of water in your tank into a bucket.

Eg: My tank is 250 litre so 30% is about 70 litres.

At the same time with the head of your syphon use it to vacuum up all the muck from the bottom. This will help keep your water pure.

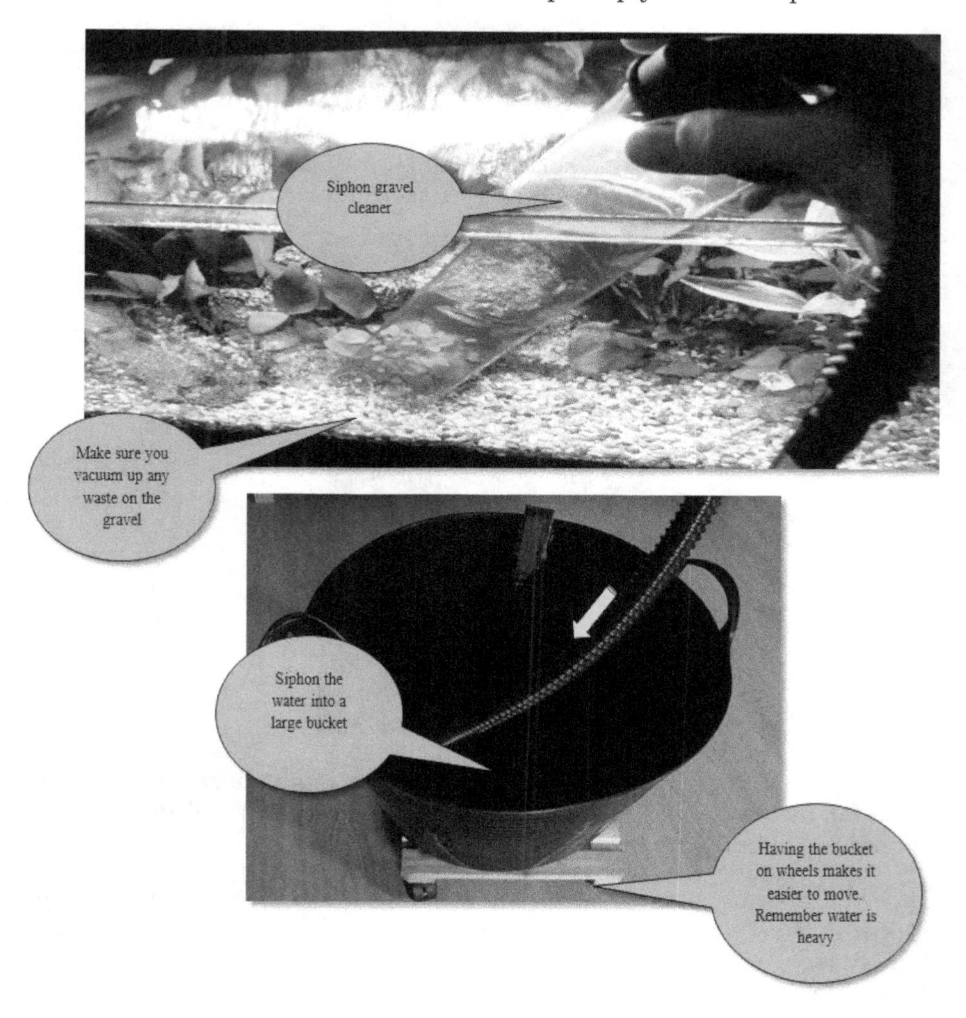

Make sure you have a bucket big enough to take all the water and remember water is heavy so be careful moving the bucket to tip the water away. Put the bucket on a sturdy trolley and use a pump to empty it down the drain or in the garden, never try to lift it.

Cleaning your Filter

Over time the sponges inside your filter will clog and this is what needs to be cleaned out regularly. I would clean it about once a month. In this cleaning guide I use a Fluval 306 but the principles can be applied to cleaning any filter.

It is a good idea to clean your filter during a water change as you will have a bucket of tank water to use.

Unhooking the Filter

If your filter allows for it block off the hoses to maintain water vacuum in the hoses. For the Fluval series of canister filters this is achieved by pulling up the grey lever on the hose attachment.

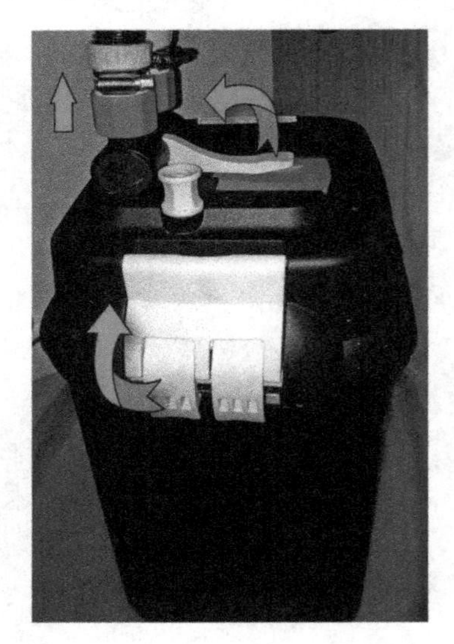

If your filter does not have this capability you might need to withdraw the filter intake from the tank otherwise your intake will draw water upon disconnection from the canister unit.

Once the hose is blocked off or the intake has been removed from the tank it is then safe to turn off power to the canister unit. Once this is done disconnect the hoses (or hose unit if you're using a Fluval) from the unit and carry the filter to the workspace.

For internal filters, unplug them from the mains power then slide the filter off the glass releasing the suction cups and place into a bucket.

Cleaning the Sponges

Set it down on a workspace open up the filter (for Fluvals this is done by lifting the two light grey clamps on either side of the unit) and have a look inside, it should look mucky like this:

First clean the sponge media as it is easily the dirtiest component of a canister filter. With the Fluval models the sponge media is attached to a tray unit. To access the media simply lift the unit as shown above.

Most manuals and fish shops recommend throwing out this media and replacing it with new media, the reason for this is money is made when you are continually buying new media. Do not do this, your tank will benefit from keeping the old media as it will contain all the necessary bacteria to remove toxins from the water.

It is IMPORTANT NEVER to use TAP WATER to clean filter components as chlorine/chloramine in the tap water will destroy your biological bacteria and render your filter useless upon reconnection.

Using your syphon fill a bucket with tank water from the aquarium and use this to rinse off the sponge media. The bucket water will get dirty fast so use additional tank water as required.

Wring the sponges out in the tank water till it is clean. Just do it enough to get rid of all the solid waste and gunk.

Once all mechanical media is cleaned leave it in some tank water do not allow it to dry out.

Rinse out the Biological Media or Ceramic Rings

In the Fluval 06 filters with the sponge media sometimes the biological filter baskets do get a decent amount of muck in them.

I would only clean the biological filter baskets if it is clogged, blocked or looks really dirty, otherwise leave it alone as you do not want to disturb the bacterial colonies that grow on the rings. This is responsible for removing the toxins from the water such as ammonia.

To clean them out gently rinse them by moving the basket up and down a few times in a bucket of tank water just enough so the solid waste falls out.

There is no need to remove all the chips. I use the same bucket of water for all three stacks of baskets.

Once rinsed simply set aside the biological media. Do not allow to dry out.

Clean the Filter Housing & Impeller Unit

Empty out the dirty water from inside the canister housing and give it a scrub with your filter sponge.

It is ok for the inside of the housing to feel slimy but remove any solid build up.

The secret to clear water is not to actually clean the filter thoroughly just to remove gunk and solid waste but retaining the bacterial colonies to purify the water.

Before attaching the propeller unit be sure to line the rubber seal with Vaseline. This prolongs the life of the seal and stops it from getting brittle over time.

After it's all assembled carry the filter unit back to the tank.

Restarting the filter

Before restarting the filter grab a clean kitchen sponge (not one that has been used for washing up as it will have soap and detergent that will poison the fish). I would keep one spare just for fish tank maintenance.

When the hoses are left for a while without a constant water flow through them gunk starts to fall off the insides and if not caught in a sponge will make your tank look horrible for a few hours after filter restart.

With the sponge over the output it's now time to prime the filter. For the Fluvals this is simply a matter of clipping the hose unit back onto the top of the filter and then pushing the black lever down. The water should start to siphon into the tank if it doesn't, you might have to pump the manual primer a few times to get it going and then water should flow until the canister is full.

For other brands the concept is the same, reconnect the hoses and prime the unit till it is full of water.

Once water stops flowing into the unit it's time to turn the filter back on. Plug in the unit and watch the outflow, water should start pouring from the sponge otherwise you might have to try a few plug/unplugs till it gets going. You can also use a sock or net.

Let the flow run for a few minutes and then carefully remove the sponge from the output hose being careful not to let the gunk captured escape into the tank.

Maintaining Live Plants

While you are changing the water is a good time to do any maintenance on your live plants. I usually do this before I fill the tank up again with fresh dechlorinated water. This makes it easier to work when the water level is lower.

Inspect your plants for any dead or dying leaves and trim them off as near to the base as possible with your long handled cutters.

Don't leave any storks with no leaves as they will just rot in the tank.

Also cut back any leaves that are growing too big etc.

Dose with a good liquid plant fertiliser if required.

Addition of CO_2

If your plants are not growing particularly well and you have sufficient light and fertilisers, then it could be due to lack of CO_2 in the water. There are a number of ways to add CO_2 and plenty of devices on the market to choose from or you can make your own CO_2 reactor.

Get yourself a litre plastic drinks bottle or soda bottle and glue a piece of silicon tubing to the cap. Best glue to use is a hot melt glue gun as it makes a non-toxic seal as shown below left.

Connect the other end of the tube to a diffuser and stick it to the glass at the bottom of the tank so the bubbles gently flow into the water as shown above right. You can buy these CO_2 diffusers from any fish store

Fill the bottle with a teaspoon of yeast and a couple of teaspoons of sugar. Then fill the bottle about 2 inches from the bottom with warm water (not boiling or hot). Put the cap on tightly and mix it around.

After a few minutes the yeast begin to convert the sugar and will start to release CO_2 into the water.

Keep an eye on your fish as too much CO_2 can cause them to become listless or even poison them.

Don't let any of that gunge at the bottom of the bottle get in the pipes or into the aquarium as it will contain alcohol and poison the fish.

Only use this when the aquarium lights are on. Don't run it when the lights are off. Plants only require CO_2 when there is light.

Preparing Fresh Water

Fill your bucket with the same amount fresh water as you took out the tank.

Remember this water is probably cold so you need to get it up to the same temperature as the water in your tank. You can do this by adding a couple of boiled kettles of water just enough to raise the temperature of the water in the bucket. Aim for about 25°C. A small mercury thermometer is handy to use here.

Once the temperature of the water is correct, add a dose of water conditioner (I use API Stress Coat) to the water in the bucket and stir. Let it stand for a few minutes.

Refilling the Tank

Now the bucket is going to be heavy, so to save you from having to lift the bucket to pour it into the tank, put your submersible pump in the bucket and hook the outlet pipe over the side of the tank.

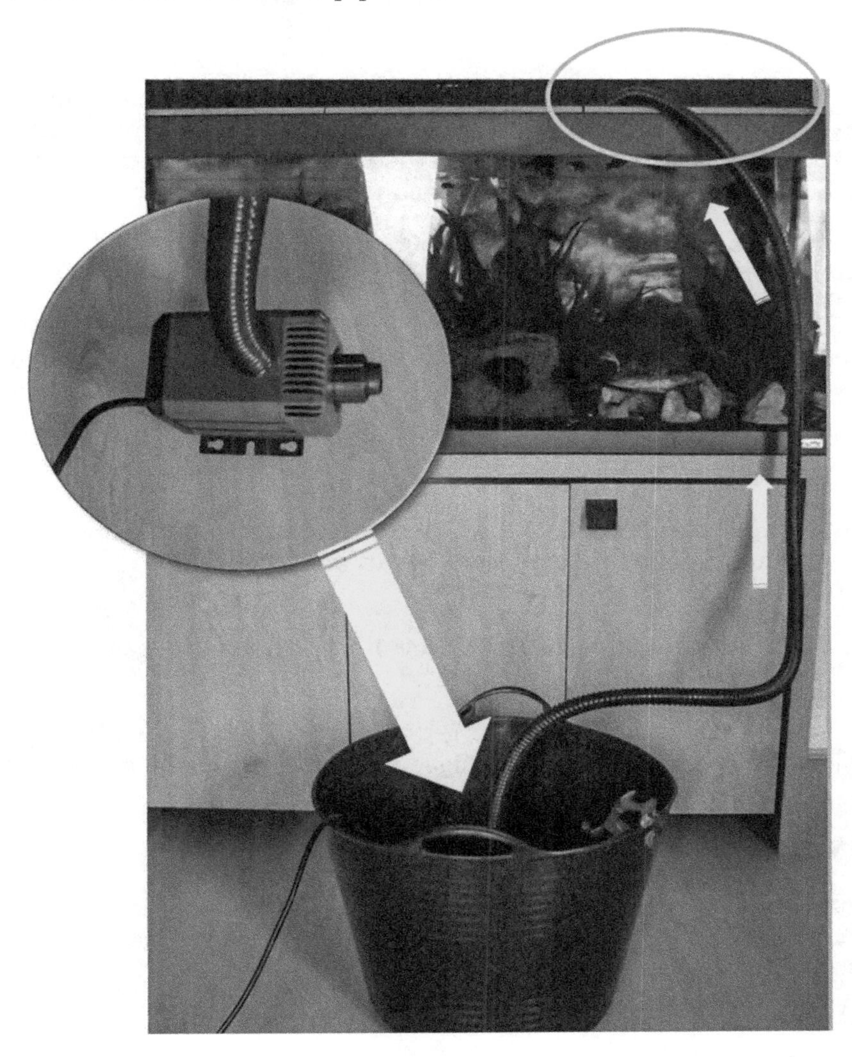

Turn on your pump and watch the water flow back into the tank. Make sure you stop the pump when the water runs out or you reach the max fill line on the tank.

For smaller tanks under 100litres try using a large watering can to prepare your water and refill the tank.

Common Problems

Most problems with an aquarium can usually be traced back to water quality.

Water Quality

If your fish are displaying symptoms such as, not eating, rapid gill movement, staying near surface, listless at bottom of tank or erratic movements, these symptoms can usually be traced back to water quality problems, such as high ammonia or high nitrite levels.

If Ammonia/Nitrite levels are high, immediately carry out a water change, up to 40% if necessary and prepare fresh conditioned water for your fish.

Check the filter to make sure it isn't blocked and make sure the filter flow is circulating around the tank.

Algae

A lot of algae can be caused by high amount of phosphate and nitrate in the water. Phosphate is present in tap water and also in some kinds of fish foods.

Brown algae is usually caused by low light and green algae is caused by direct sunlight or too much light.

Try some phosphate remover or get yourself a bristlenose plec if your tank is big enough. Also try an algae magnet to clean the glass.

Plants

Poor colour, leaves falling off or yellow spots on the leaves can be due to a lack of iron. This can happen after a few months of planting as the plants deplete the nutrients in the planting substrate. A good liquid fertilizer will help solve the problem.

Can also be due to lack of CO_2 and light.

Common Disease

Maintaining a clean tank, with regular water changes and maintenance to achieve crystal clear water with 0 ammonia and 0 nitrite is the best preventative precaution to your fish getting sick. However if they do get sick the infections are usually bacterial, fungal or parasitic.

Bacterial Infections: Inactivity, loss of colour, frayed fins, bloated body, cloudy eyes, open sores, abscesses, red streaks throughout body, reddening or inflammation of the skin, fins or internal organs, bulging eyes, difficulty breathing.

Fungal Infections (often secondary to another type of illness): Erratic swimming, darting, scratching, visible cotton-like tufts on skin, eyes, or mouth.

Parasitic Infections: Inactivity, loss of appetite, excess mucus or film on body, visible spots or worms, rapid breathing, scratching.

The following two tables are some symptoms of some of the more common diseases.

Please note that this is a guide and you should read all the labels on the medication to make sure it is treating the correct disease and to make sure that the medication is applied correctly and in the correct dose. Incorrectly used medication can be lethal to your fish.

Symptoms	Possible Diagnosis	Treatment
Greyish-white film on skin, damaged fins, ulcers, yellow to grey patches on gills, tissue on head may be eaten away.	Columnaris (Cotton Wool Disease)	Must be treated immediately with Over-the-counter antibiotic medications. Very contagious disinfect tank, rocks, net, etc.
Swelling of head, bulging eyes.	Corneybacteriosis	OTC antibiotics such as penicillin and tetracycline.
Swelling of abdomen, raised scales around swollen area.	Dropsy (Malawi Bloat) may be caused by internal bacterial infection (if swelling is sudden), parasites, or cancer (if swelling is gradual).	Add 1/8 teaspoon of Epsom salt for every 5 gallons of water and monitor for two weeks. Check for signs of bacterial infection or parasites for further treatment.
Ragged or decaying fins.	Fin rot	Check pH and correct as needed. If level is normal, use OTC antibiotic for fin or tail rot.
Erratic swimming, bloating or swelling in body, black patches on body or fins.	Myxobacteriosis -- rare	Medications, if any, are difficult to come by. Keep up on water maintenance to prevent it.
White or grey fungus on eyes.	Cataracts	OTC medication for fungus.
White or grey patches resembling cotton, excess mucus.	Mouth or Body Fungus	OTC medication for fungus. Usually added to water, but may need direct application.
White cotton-like patches on fins, body, or mouth.	True Fungus (Saprolegnia)	OTC medication for fungus. Check for symptoms of other illnesses.
Small string-like worms visible on fish, or burrowed in skin.	Anchor Worm	Over-the-counter medication for parasites.
Weight loss, strained breathing.	Copepods	OTC medication for parasites, also fungal treatment for possible secondary infection on damaged gills
White film, reddened areas on body, abnormal swimming, scratching, folded fins.	Costia (Slime Disease)	Must be treated quickly. Raise water temperature and use OTC medication for parasites. Salt treatment may work, as well.
Sluggishness, flashing, spider web lesions on skin, colour loss, reddened fins, drooping fins, fin damage.	Skin Flukes (Gyrodactylus)	OTC medication for parasites
Lack of appetite, weight loss, small holes or eroding pits appearing in the head.	Hole in Head Disease (Hexamita) more common in cichlids	OTC medication for Hole in Head Disease.
Scratching, white salt-like spots starting on head and spreading over whole body, rapid breathing, and cloudiness on eyes or fins.	Ich (Ichtyophthirius) very common	OTC medication for Ich or Ick.
Scratching, small worms hanging from body.	Leech	Salt treatment or OTC medication for parasites.
Erratic swimming, weight loss, loss of colour.	Neon Tetra Disease mostly affects tetras, danios, and barbs	Treatment is difficult look for a medication that treats gram-negative bacteria or with nalidixic acid as the active ingredient.

Darting, scratching, small yellow to white spots dusting skin.	Oodinium	OTC treatment for parasites.
Cloudy appearance on skin, red patches on skin where parasite has bitten.	Trichodina -- predominately freshwater	Salt treatment.
Red or bloody gills, gasping for air.	Ammonia Poisoning	No treatment. Regular water testing and maintenance will prevent it.
Small dark spots on fins and body.	Black Spot	OTC medication for parasites. Spots (cysts) may remain after treatment.
Cloudy white appearance to one or both eyes.	Cloudy Eye	Check for symptoms of another illness like velvet, ich, or tuberculosis. Treat with OTC medication.
String of faeces hanging from fish, swollen abdomen, sluggishness, disinterest in food, off-balance swimming.	Constipation	Stop feeding for 2-3 days and continue with a more varied diet including live and plant-based foods.
Small white spots that get larger over time possibly with black streaks.	Fish Pox	No treatment. Keep up on water maintenance and symptoms should cease after about 10-12 weeks.
Reddening on or under skin, sudden abnormal behaviour.	Inflammation	OTC antibiotic treatment.
Unusual bulging of one or both eyes.	Pop-eye (Exophthalmia)	OTC medication for bacterial infections and/or parasites. Check for other symptoms of bacterial or parasitic infections.
Fish struggles to swim, may float with head tipped down, or have difficulty surfacing, no balance, etc. May occur after eating.	Swim Bladder Disease	Stop feeding for 3-4 days. If symptoms persist, feed the affected fish a small amount of fresh spinach or a green pea without the skin (laxatives).
Swelling or distention for internal tumours, external can be seen growing on skin.	Tumours	Usually incurable. Consult a veterinarian about potassium iodide treatment for thyroid tumours.
Sluggishness, lack of appetite, open sores with red edges, possible fin rot.	Ulcers	OTC medication for bacterial infections.
Scratching, small gold to white spots, loss of colour, weight loss, difficulty breathing due to gill damage.	Velvet (Gold Dust Disease)	OTC medication for parasites

Maintenance Tips

As a guide daily, weekly, monthly and annual checklist have been included here as a suggestion to the steps required to maintain a healthy fish tank. You can use as a general guide to keeping your aquarium in top shape.

Also included are suggestions and tips on light levels required by some plants to survive.

Plus a few example equariums with different layouts, fish, plants, etc for you to see.

Daily Routine

Observe your tank closely at least once a day. While you're enjoying the view, take note of a few things.

Temperature

Check heater to make sure it's still working. Keep an eye on the thermometer and ensure it's still at the correct temperature for your fish.

Water Level

Top off evaporated water when the level starts to drop. If you do regular water changes then this shouldn't be a problem

Unusual Behaviour

New fish may take a while to settle into normal behaviour. Recent changes such as a new addition to the tank can cause shifts in normal behaviour. But most of the time, fish are pretty consistent.

Dead Fish or Organisms

Small fish that like to hide in decorations or rock crevices could easily die and be unnoticed for days. A dead organism immediately begins to decompose and will soon flood your system with toxic ammonia,

Weekly Routine

During a weekly or biweekly cleaning routine, you should clean algae and debris from your tank and gravel, and doing your water change.

Water Change/Cleaning Routine

As mentioned in chapter 6 Siphon off 20-30% of your water. Using a bucket or a water changer that feeds into a sink are the usual methods.

Don't discard water immediately if you intend to rinse mechanical filter media of debris, or rinse ornaments.

Leave your fish in the aquarium - moving them is more stressful than a water change.

Use an algae scraper or scrubber to remove any dirt or algae that's accumulated on your tank walls.

If you have live plants, it's a great time to prune, re-anchor, and remove any dead bits.

Using a gravel vacuum or siphon, suck particles of debris ("mulm") from your gravel and anything floating in your water.

Stir the gravel or sand lightly with your siphon as you go.

Monthly Routine

During the monthly routine, you should test/check equipment such as filters and the water flow. Check your water parameters using a test kit and clean your filter.

Testing Equipment

Test pH levels, ammonia, nitrites and nitrates and keep records of the results, days and times that you took them. (pH varies throughout the day, so measuring at the same time matters.)

Check the water is flowing out of the filter, make sure it isn't reduced flow or a blocked filter.

Clean Filter

Biological media should only be rinsed if it is clogged with debris, but never rinse a significant portion at once.

A light film of slime shouldn't be cause for concern. Biological media normally doesn't need to be replaced, and shouldn't be.

Rinse pads and sponges in aquarium water - do this during a water change, so you can use the water you removed from the tank. If they are so clogged they can't be cleaned, it's time to replace them.

When you clean your media, observe the inside of your filter components - if there is a lot of gunk clogging up the works, remove it with a flexible cleaning brush.

Annual Routine

Checking lights, pumps, filters, seals, impellers etc.

Light Bulbs/ UV Bulbs

Unless stated otherwise by the manufacturer, light bulbs and UV lamps usually need to be replaced every six months. Even if you see light, wavelengths of the original spectrum gradually decay, so your aquarium isn't getting "daylight" anymore.

Changing bulbs at night is easier - it allows lamps to cool before you have to handle them, and you won't have to disrupt your tank's normal photo-period.

For light intensive systems that use multiple lamps, change out lamps one at a time over a period of days - the sudden heightened intensity can be a shock to organisms.

Never touch a metal halide lamp with your fingers even when cool; use a glove. The oils from your fingers weaken the glass and with such intense heating, could cause an explosion.

Pumps, Filters

If you're starting out, you may want to check pumps and filters every three months at first - depending on your bioload or how many fish you have, they may need cleaning more often than twice a year. But for many systems, it should be adequate.

Pumps and filters house a motor and impeller which is part of the filter that drives the water around. To clean them, remove the impeller, clean debris from it and its housing. If the impeller is missing blades or is cracked, replace it.

Clean all housings, intake and outlet pipes and the body of the filter or pump. You may need a filter or tubing brush to get all the way inside these parts, but don't skimp out on this cleaning - after all, it has to get you through the next half of the year.

Lubricate moving parts and rubber seals with Vaseline

Reassemble and reinstall. Some filters and pumps need to be primed before they will start.

Plant Lighting Requirements

As mentioned earlier in the book

Low lights are between 1 - 2 watts per US gallon (0.3 - 0.5 watt/litre)

Medium lights are between 2 - 3 watts per US gallon (0.5 - 0.8 watt/litre)

High lights have 3 watts per US gallon or higher (0.8 watt/litre or higher)

Here are some common species of plants and the types of lighting levels they need to survive.

You may also need to consider what fish you are keeping as very bright lights can cause them stress.

Low Light

- Anubias species
- Cryptocoryne species (most)
- Echinodorous species - Amazon swords (some)
- Microsorium pteropus (Java Fern)
- Vesicularia dubyana (Java Moss)

Bright Light

- Aponogeton species
- Ceratopteris thalictroides (Indian fern)
- Crinum species
- Egeria densa (Waterweed)
- Hygrophila difformis (Water wisteria)
- Hygrophila polysperma (Giant/green/Indian Hygrophila)
- Lilaeopsis species
- Limnophila species
- Ludwigia species
- Myriophyllum species
- Nesaea species
- Nymphaea stellata (Water lily)
- Pogostemon species
- Rotala species
- Sagittaria species
- Vallisneria species

Index

F

G

H

I

L

M

N

O